Si 6.2:Sa 3

WITHDRAWN

Si 6.2:Sa 3

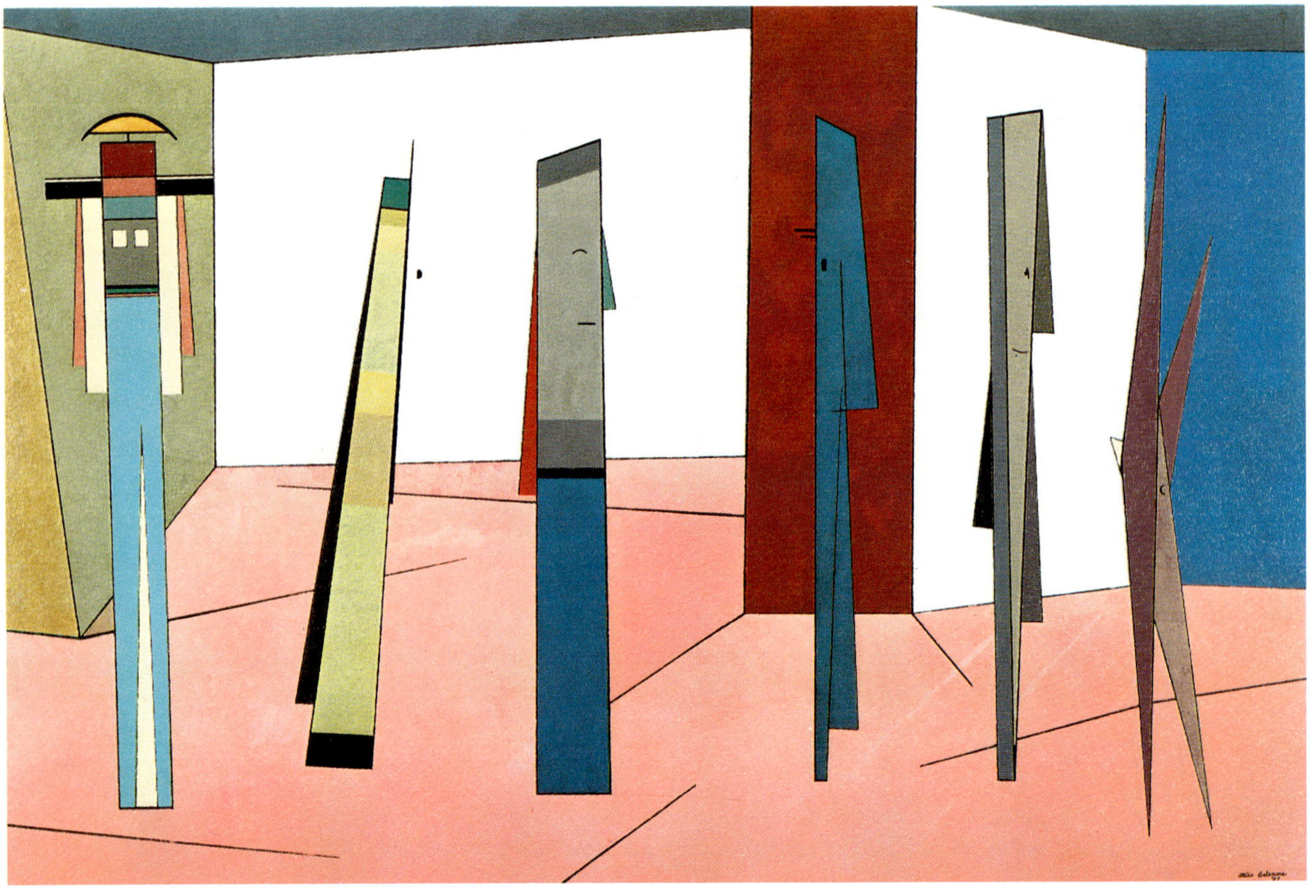

ATTILIO SALEMME
Inhabitant of a Dream

Published for the **NATIONAL COLLECTION OF FINE ARTS**

by the **SMITHSONIAN INSTITUTION PRESS,** *City of Washington, 1978*

Published on the occasion of an exhibition at the National Collection of Fine Arts, Smithsonian Institution, Washington, D.C., March 3-May 7, 1978, and The Solomon R. Guggenheim Museum, New York, New York, June 23-August 6, 1978.

Cover: *Into the Night,* 1949, catalogue number 28.
Frontispiece: *Enigma of Joy,* 1947, catalogue number 17.

Photographic Credits

Oliver Baker: catalogue numbers 1, 5, 10, 17, 18, 20, 21, 22, 24, 27, 29, 30, 31, 37, 39, 40, 41, 43, 45, 47.
Geoffrey Clements: catalogue number 25.   Fred A. Hamel: catalogue numbers 2, 6, 13, 33, 38, 46, 48, 49.
Robert E. Mates: catalogue number 44.   Robert E. Mates and Mary Donlon: catalogue numbers 19, 34.
Ethel Pries: page 8.   Percy Rainford: catalogue number 7.   Walter Rosenblum: catalogue numbers 28, 35.

For Sale by the Superintendent of Documents, United States Government Printing Office, Washington, D.C. 20402,
Stock number: 047-003-00059-8

CONTENTS

7 **FOREWORD** *Joshua C. Taylor*

9 **ATTILIO SALEMME: INHABITANT OF A DREAM** *Adelyn D. Breeskin*

15 **CHRONOLOGY** *Julie Link Haifley*

17 **ONE-MAN EXHIBITIONS**

17 **GROUP EXHIBITIONS**

19 **REFERENCES**

21 **LENDERS TO THE EXHIBITION**

23 **CATALOGUE OF THE EXHIBITION**

Library of Congress Cataloging in Publication Data

Smithsonian Institution. National Collection of Fine Arts.
Attilio Salemme.

Catalog of an exhibition held at the National Collection of Fine Arts, Smithsonian Institution, March 3-May 7, 1978, and at the Solomon R. Guggenheim Museum, New York, June 23-August 6, 1978 catalog prepared by A. D. Breeskin, chronology and bibliography by J. L. Haifley.

Bibliography: p. 19
1. Salemme, Attilio, 1911——Exhibitions
I. Breeskin, Adelyn Dohme, 1896— II. Haifley, Julia Link.
ND237.S25A4 1978   759.13   78-3541

FOREWORD

Attilio Salemme was an artist who quickly made his mark and equally quickly, it seemed, disappeared from the scene. His painting career was brief—hardly more than twelve years—yet he remains as a distinct artistic personality with a quality quite his own.

Salemme served only a brief apprenticeship in art. Reflecting the extraordinary range and artistic sophistication available in New York City in the late 1930s, his earliest efforts were knowing and adroit. To judge from his early works he was nurtured on Cézanne and his followers, early took abstraction for granted, and refined his nice sense for formal humor and surprise on the works of Paul Klee. The spirit of Carlo Carrà and other painters of the *Scuola Metafisica* was not lost on him, and like others he cherished that sense of loneliness and detachment which was fashionably called a kind of aesthetic alienation. To be alone in art was to join the modern community.

Into the sensitive modern world of waiting space he introduced his own cast of characters, slim angular constructions of forms which acted for all the world as if they were the national inhabitants of their rarefied artistic lair. They chat, scowl, charm, and terrify, touch without making contact and talk without being heard. Salemme regarded mankind from the inside, not from appearance, and there is little in his strange rooms and empty landscapes that recalls specific phenomena. Yet his people and places, never before seen, all seem familiar as if we have known them all along. Out of a few modernist angles he created an unrepeatable but memorable language, speaking of particular human values in a generalized world.

We are grateful to Lucia Salemme for making the works of her late husband that remain in her possession available to us for the present exhibition. Although Salemme's works are included in many museum collections, there has been little opportunity in recent years to appreciate the range and adroitness of his works as seen together. Mrs. Salemme has been helpful in all phases of the exhibition, including putting us in contact with private owners of Salemme's paintings. We are much indebted to the individuals and museums who have lent works from their collections and deeply appreciate their generous cooperation.

Works for the exhibition were selected and the catalogue prepared by Adelyn D. Breeskin, our consultant in Twentieth Century Painting and Sculpture; Julie Link Haifley of the Office of Program Support prepared the chronology and bibliography. The installation of the exhibition was thoughtfully conceived and designed by Val Lewton and executed under the Office of Exhibition and Design directed by David Keeler.

Joshua C. Taylor
Director
National Collection of Fine Arts

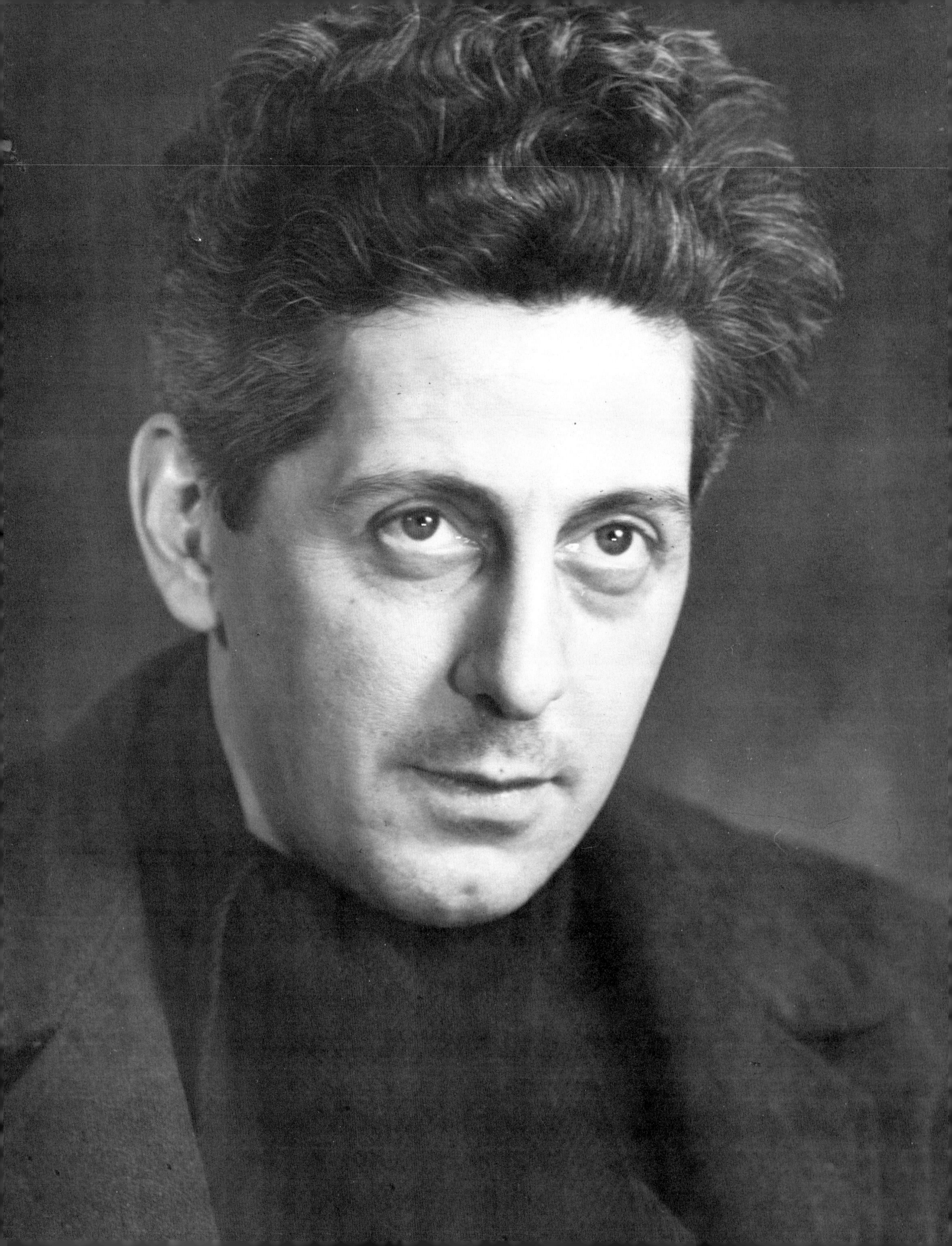

ATTILIO SALEMME Inhabitant of a Dream

Attilio Salemme came late to painting, having first tried his hand at a variety of pursuits. Once he began, however, he quickly found his personal means of expression and remained consistent in his vision until his untimely death in 1955. He was born in Brookline, Massachusetts, in 1911 and—his father having died when his son was only five years old—worked hard as a youth to help in the support of his mother and sister. Before he reached the age of eighteen he had joined the United States Marine Corps, having falsified the date of his birth, and was stationed for over six months in Port-au-Prince, Haiti. He later recalled Haiti as having an unforgettable, magical quality. On his discharge from the Marine Corps in 1928, he had difficulty in readjusting to civilian life and could find only menial work by which to earn a living. In 1930 he moved with his mother and sister to New York City and became acquainted with the life in Greenwich Village. He also went to night school, where he studied diligently. For some time he thought that he would study to become a chemical engineer. Finally, however, in 1938 he pawned a rifle left from his time in the Marines and bought a set of paints. He first painted a group of still lifes and later a few landscapes. An unsuccessful venture in establishing a ceramic kiln for artists diverted him from painting, and he went off to Boston for six months to read Plato and to decide on his future. Upon his return he became distraught over the impending new world war, was found by his half-brother in need of help from a nervous breakdown, and consequently spent six months in a state hospital.

During the years in which Salemme was discovering art, much was happening in the art world of New York. Although many artists had been convinced of the need for a socially conscious art—and Salemme for a time considered himself a revolutionary—by the end of the 1930s there was a turn toward more introspective concerns. The ideas of the surrealists were much discussed, as were religious and psychological concepts. Salemme became interested in early cultures and read with intensity works pertaining to the ancient world. He seems to have shared with others the desire to belong to a society with deep, mythical roots, quite different from the urban commercial culture in which he lived.

Salemme's acquaintance with the world of art in New York was advanced by a special circumstance: he became the framemaker for the Solomon R. Guggenheim Foundation's Museum of Non-Objective Painting. There, for the first time, he met congenial people who were interested in what meant so much to him. Clearly he became fascinated with the militant program of the gallery under Hilla Rebay in promoting nonobjective art as a modern inevitability, and doubtless saw much that was meaningful in the later works by Kandinsky as well as in works by lesser painters who stressed universal meaning in dynamic, geometrical compositions. But Salemme tended to see beings where others were inclined to see only cosmic patterns.

Not until 1943 did Salemme believe that he had achieved what he was after in painting. Most of his forms were drawn with draftsmanly precision, one plane overlapping another with diagonals and verticals locked in a nicely balanced equilibrium. Yet for all of the seemingly impersonal objectivity, small clues transform what

Attilio Salemme in 1948 at age thirty-eight.

otherwise would be considered nonobjective shapes into discreet personalities. Strangely, nothing actually looks like a being in Salemme's painting, yet there is a hint that shut up within the isolated, rigid shapes there is a creatural desire to communicate.

Salemme was obsessed with the threat of human isolation, with the pulling back from experiment and exploration. "Life has infinite doors to beckon with and each day reveals new doors," he wrote. "Men continue to pass through these doors. We live in an age when men are no longer content with discovering new doors but have begun to close them and to erect them around themselves. But there is no escape from the door that all doors lead to."[1] So he set out to surprise his viewers with a discovery of promised human activity in nonhuman circumstances, often wittingly destroying rational confines after encouraging the mind to be rational. For all of their gaiety of color and wit, however, and for all of the jaunty, distinctive character realized in each sticklike form, there is a feeling of separateness in the works that is seldom, if ever, overcome. It is as if the tensions of society are expressed in the tension between his pylonlike figures. The longer one looks, the more complex the subjects become. In spite of protestations of detached nonobjectivity, the paintings often hint at a loneliness that Giorgio de Chirico earlier called a metaphysical solitude. They operate in an unsettling, tragicomic mode.

"People," he said, "are the subject of my painting; what they are doing is usually indicated by the titles."[2] Salemme's titles reveal a particularly thoughtful mind. From *The First Communication* of 1943 and *Atavistic Premonition* (cat. no. 9) of 1944 to *Lunar Voyage* (cat. no. 44) of 1954, the titles make clear that the associative overtones one senses are not matters of chance or unconcern. "...I can catalogue the paintings," he wrote, "and reduce my feelings and thoughts to a simple verbalization that sums up the experience in a kind of elementary, non-pictorial articulation—a reference that is both a spring-board and a frame of accomplishment."[3] To Salemme, in whatever form art takes, "the end is always the same—the extension of one's self in time by the act of creation."[4]

Yet, it is not in the suggestive titles but in the neatly drawn forms sharing in a void that the content of the paintings lies. The words play in a kind of counterpoint with the visual activity. The two forces together become the symbol. For Salemme, however, it was the visual form that carried the chief burden of meaning. "Symbolism is the very most precise way of representing an idea, person or thing,"[5] he said. But the symbolism of painting is precise only in the form it takes in the painting: it cannot be translated into words without losing its precision.

Most of Salemme's titles, of course, are no more profusely descriptive than his paintings. Such titles as *Caught in the Equinox* (cat. no. 43) and *Atavistic Premonition* set a direction or climate for thought without fixing on a particular object or incident. They at once suggest, however, that the spacial emptiness has a meaning quite beyond normal dimensions. In *Atavistic Premonition* of 1944, for example, the precariously balanced upright forms seem drawn by an irresistible magnetism to the one solid volume in the painting, the pyramid. The space is charged with a mysterious current that sustains the floating splinters that people the lonely void. Only the slightest hint is needed—such as two well-placed dots—for the viewer to identify himself with the mesmerized shapes. In using a pyramid as the center of sustaining force, Salemme was not necessarily suggesting that Egypt is the actual source of ancestral premonitions, but through association the pyramid transforms the strange tension in space into a parable of time. As a youth in Boston, Salemme often visited the Egyptian galleries at the museum and was particularly awed by the powerful sculptures with their self-contained sense of being and air of remoteness. Later he read as much as he could find about the Egyptians and their concern

The artist and his wife Lucia, 1945.

for the perpetuation of life in the face of death. Like many drawn to the enigmatic beauty of Egyptian art, he seems to have been moved by it because it offered a personal contact with an ancient, mysterious source. Yet in his painting the references to life, to a Jungian force, to the precarious situation of man, or simply to his own fascination with Egypt are as understated as his sparse forms. Possibly he followed the principle that the slighter the pictorial hint the freer the imagination is to respond.

Salemme had a nice sense for environmental suggestion and was attentive to the situation of man as seen in terms of universal functions. Like Paul Klee he could become acutely aware of the personal and individual as a contrasting element to the large cycles of nature. Speaking of his painting *Caught in the Equinox,* he wrote, "It is my personal conviction that the light during the vernal and autumnal equinox is quite different from all other days of the year—the idea of being 'caught' in the equinox is an attempt to arrest by an image the force of inarticulate feelings and ideas that slumber deeply rooted in my atavistic past of this most important astronomical event."[6] Significantly, the painting was finished on September 23, 1953, the day of the autumnal equinox and his wife Lucia's birthday.

Of a very different nature is the painting entitled *The Inquisition* (cat. no. 39). Rather than presenting a quietly haunting situation it develops its theme almost histrionically, treating of man's relationship to man instead of to his ancient past or to seasonal change. "In the guise of some ideas or dogma," he wrote, "a relentless struggle is dramatized. The result is never a clearcut victory of one over the other but the achievement is always an increase of pain and misery compounded of distrust, confusion and suspicion." He went on to describe his austere figures, which seem to carry with them their own architecture, as actors in a tragic play: "The ritual of the drama is presented by a formal court of symbolic personages headed by a deadly character standing on a path that leads past a tombstone to a wall. If I have succeeded in creating the feeling that once we are on this path there is no unmaimed escape, then I think I have communicated my antipathy to all inquisitions—past, present and future."[7]

Lunar Voyage of 1954 (well before, it should be noted, lunar voyages became a reality) affords a flight into a clear, free atmosphere that is both awesome and welcome. One feels the coldness and whiteness beyond. There are the usual guardian figures but they are not oppressive as in *The Inquisition.* Lines move upward and the reaching central figure is free and buoyant in space, even though the atmosphere is bleak and frigid. Recalling the weeks during which he was at work on the painting, he said, "I was fortunately not obsessed with it to the exclusion of all else." As for the thoughts that prompted it, he stated, "The thoughts that I recall are . . . best articulated by painting; were it otherwise I might find myself more interested in writing or music and then . . . I might be incapable of articulating anything more than a lunar binge."[8] A binge his painting is not; it is an exceedingly refined and polished formal statement.

Refinement and polish did not necessarily spell solemnity and awe to Salemme. He delighted in a restrained formal wit. Some of his slim, shadowless planar figures are coquettish, shy, and almost chatty. Madame X (cat. no. 50) is quite naughty, and Adam and Eve (cat. no. 46) seem to be eager but empty vessels from Mars.

Salemme's style began to take form when he set out to write a dictionary of art terms for artists. He wanted to define *what is a line?, what is a curve?* but found himself drawing the answers instead of writing about them. He became so absorbed in the project that he concentrated on it for an entire year to the exclusion of everything else. He then started to create compositions with figures that were to form the principal elements in his works throughout his all too short career as a painter. His sensitivity to the slight variations of a line or shape was extraordinarily acute, and he lived every line he drew. At their freest they could dance and gesture with fragile

Attilio Salemme circa 1954.

abandon, as in the *Dawn Ballet* (cat. no. 34) of 1951. When disciplined with almost mechanical regularity they could be as primly uncomfortable as a small boy in a Sunday suit, or austerely grand and often threatening. His range of expression through a deliberately limited formal means was continuously astonishing.

Although critics have found parallels between Salemme's painting and that of Giorgio de Chirico, Ives Tanguy, Paul Klee, and Piet Mondrian, the fact remains that Salemme's art was very much his own. To be sure, he drew upon the idiom of his time, but his curiously poignant, sometimes humorous, sometimes terrifying statements remain unique. Thomas Messer, who gave Salemme his first museum exhibition, remarked that there was a quality in his work akin to that found in the writings of Franz Kafka. In both there is a feeling of estrangement, human loss, guilt, and anxiety. They both combine the recognizable and the mysterious, and both are afflicted with melancholy and the feverish imaginings of a captive hemmed in by his own existence. In both Salemme and Kafka there is also the desire to attain the pure, the true, the immutable in their art.

The tributes that were paid to Salemme after his death were many and deeply impressive, coming from such friends as Alexander Calder, Marcel Duchamp, and Lloyd Goodrich. Particularly revealing was the statement made by Andrew Ritchie, who was then director of the Museum of Modern Art in New York:

"When I last saw Attilio in his studio. . . he did feel, he told me, that he had resolved most of the particular spatial and color problems he had been working on for so long and that his paintings had now achieved the balance and clarity he had been seeking. And certainly, for me, the evidence was there before my eyes in painting after painting." [9]

Adelyn D. Breeskin, *Consultant,*
Twentieth Century Painting and Sculpture,
National Collection of Fine Arts

Notes

All notes but numbers 4 and 9 are taken from the Attilio Salemme Papers, Archives of American Art, Smithsonian Institution.
1. From Salemme's application for a Guggenheim Fellowship, 1945, Section 3: "Philosophy, principles and aims of art."
2. Attilio Salemme to Miss Wagenet, March 23, 1947.
3. Attilio Salemme to Edwin C. Rae, University of Illinois, November 11, 1954.
4. Comment by the artist in the catalogue for his one-man exhibition at the 67 Gallery, New York, 1945.
5. Attilio Salemme to John Entenza, *Art and Architecture,* March 21, 1949.
6. Excerpt from a letter to Abe Chanin, June 21, 1954.
7. Excerpt from a letter to Abe Chanin, June 21, 1954.
8. Attilio Salemme to Edwin C. Rae, University of Illinois, November 11, 1954.
9. Statement by Andrew C. Ritchie in *Attilio Salemme 1911-1955,* catalogue of an exhibition at the Duveen-Graham Gallery, New York, 1955.

CHRONOLOGY

Julie Link Haifley

1911   Born in Brookline, Massachusetts, October 18. Son of Vincenzo Salemme and Maria Branzetti.

1913   Birth of sister, Lydia.

1916   Father died.

1926   Graduated from junior high school in Boston and began working at odd jobs to help support his mother and sister. Studied Etruscan, Greek, and Egyptian collections in Boston Museum of Fine Arts.

1927   Enlisted in United States Marine Corps; served six months in Port au Prince, Haiti. Impressed by people and climate of Haiti, "its mystery, its deep, rich life of color and the magic potency that pervaded the most hum-drum activity."

1928   Received honorable discharge from United States Marine Corps. Experienced difficulty in readjusting to civilian life.

1928-1930   Held a variety of odd jobs in Boston. Visited his half-brother, sculptor Antonio Salemme, in New York City. Received from Antonio enough money to seek employment in Midwest. Unsuccessful in finding work, eventually returned to Boston penniless and disheartened.

1930-1937   Moved to New York City with his mother and sister. Helped to support self and family with odd jobs, which later included working as a laborer on early WPA projects.

Became acquainted with life and people of Greenwich Village; frequently visited Metropolitan Museum of Art.

Attended high school at night, with view to becoming chemist. Studied algebra, geometry, trigonometry, chemistry, and physics. Taught chemistry in Adult Education Division of WPA.

Discouraged by difficulties involved in becoming chemist, gave up idea and became immersed in politics. "I studied, discussed, ate, slept and dreamed the revolution night and day. . . . I quit politics at the end of 1937, convinced that the second world war was around the corner and nothing could stop it."

1938   "One day . . . I pawned a rifle which I had been saving for the revolution and bought a set of paints, determined to find out if painting was the thing I had been running away from all my life." Built kiln with sculptor friend to earn living by firing work for students, sculptors, and art schools. Had little time to paint until venture with kiln failed.

1939-1940   Spent six months in Boston reading the Greek classics and contemplating his future. Supported self with menial jobs.

Returned to New York City. Continued to read and painted a few still lifes.

1941-1942   Could not reconcile himself to impending involvement of United States in World War II. Fervently advocated a religious revolution to change the world. Became increasingly distraught and was hospitalized for five months.

Worked first as welder at Brooklyn Navy Yard, and then as framemaker at Museum of Non-Objective Painting. First exposed to modern art and met artists whom he found congenial. Exhibited one painting in group show there.

Read and studied history of Egyptian, Greco-Roman, and Judeo-Christian cultures.

1943 "... after six months of drawing, writing, and thinking about form and line, I made the first painting which I considered completely my own, evolved from the values of my experience and study."

Married painter Lucia Autorino, September 26. Shared with wife responsibility of earning a living so that each could have time to paint.

1944 Painting, *The Inescapable Consciousness,* chosen for competitive exhibition at Art of This Century gallery.

1945 First one-man exhibition at Howard Putzel's 67 Gallery.

J. J. Sweeney purchased painting, *The First Communication,* for Museum of Modern Art.

1946 Son Vincent born March 27 in New York City.

1947 Received purchase prize for silkscreen print, *One Against Many,* at First National Print Annual, Brooklyn Museum.

Received Flora Mayer Witkowsky Prize for painting, *The Astronomical Experiment,* at the "58th Annual Exhibition" of Art Institute of Chicago.

Commissioned by designer Donald Deskey to execute painting for cabin-class lounge of S.S. *Argentina* of Moore-McCormack Lines. Painting entitled *Enigma of Joy.*

1949 Established himself in large studio at 112 West Twenty-first Street.

Traveled to California in attempt to exhibit and sell his work on the West Coast, but met with little success.

1950 Represented in United States section at XXV Venice Biennale.

Metropolitan Museum of Art purchased painting, *Night of the Ritual,* from national competitive exhibition, "American Painting Today, 1950." *(Night of the Ritual later exchanged for Caught in the Equinox.)*

1951 Commissioned by architects Mayer and Whittlesey to execute two large murals for roof solarium of Manhattan House, a New York luxury apartment building. Murals entitled *In the Mirror of the Sea* and *Fra Angelico.*

Son Lawrence born September 1 in New York City.

1952 Museum of Modern Art purchased painting, *Antechamber to Inner Sanctum.*

Traveled to California again, attempting to sell work.

1953 Whitney Museum of American Art purchased painting, *The Inquisition.*

1954 Awarded grant from William and Noma Copley Foundation for achievement in field of painting.

1955 Died of a heart attack January 24 in New York City.

Brooklyn Museum purchased his painting *Tomorrow.*

ONE-MAN EXHIBITIONS

1945 67 Gallery, New York City
1946 Winfield Gallery, New York City
1947 Julius Carlebach Gallery, New York City
1948 Passedoit Gallery, New York City
1952 Saidenberg Gallery, New York City
1953 Grace Borgenicht Gallery, New York City
1955 Duveen-Graham Gallery, New York City
1959 Institute of Contemporary Art, Boston, Retrospective Exhibition. Traveled to Walker Art Center, Minneapolis, and Whitney Museum of American Art, New York City.
1960 Viviano gallery, New York City
1962 Staempfli gallery, New York City
1968 Terry Dintenfass gallery, New York City
1969 Terry Dintenfass gallery, New York City
1974 André Emmerich Gallery, New York City

GROUP EXHIBITIONS

1942 Museum of Non-Objective Painting, New York City
1943 Museum of Non-Objective Painting, New York City
1944 Art of This Century gallery, New York City, Spring Salon for Young Artists
New Art Circle gallery, New York City
1945 Albany Institute of History and Art, N.Y., "American Drawing Annual V"
David Porter Gallery, Washington, D.C. "Art in 1950: A Painting Prophecy", traveled to San Francisco Museum of Art; Wooster Museum, Ohio; City of St. Louis Museum
Outlines gallery, Pittsburgh
1946 The Museum of Modern Art traveling exhibition, "New Watercolours and Gouaches"; traveled to fourteen places
Virginia Museum of Fine Arts, Richmond
Whitney Museum of American Art, New York City, Annual Exhibition
1947 The Art Institute of Chicago, Fifty-eighth Annual Exhibition
Artists Gallery, New York City
The Brooklyn Museum, N.Y., First National Print Annual; traveled under auspices of the American Federation of Arts
Corcoran Gallery of Art, Washington, D.C., Biennial Exhibition
Fieldston School, New York City, "Paintings by Lucia Autorino and Attilio Salemme"
Julius Carlebach Gallery, New York City
The Toledo Museum of Art, Ohio
Whitney Museum of American Art, New York City, Annual Exhibition
Wildenstein Gallery, New York City, Annual Exhibition
1948 Joint Anti-Fascist Refugee Appeal, Hollywood, California. "6th Annual Art Exhibit and Sale For Hollywood"
Walker Art Center, Minneapolis, "Paintings to Know and Buy"
Whitney Museum of American Art, New York City, Annual Exhibition
1949 Rothko Gallery, New York City

Sidney Janis Gallery, "Post-Mondrian Painters in America, 1949"

Whitney Museum of American Art, New York City, Annual Exhibition

1950 Gallery Hacker, New York City

The Metropolitan Museum of Art, New York City, National Competitive Exhibition, "American Painting Today"

Passedoit Gallery, New York City

Rothko Gallery, New York City, "New Talent"

Venice Biennale, Italy, United States Exhibition

Whitney Museum of American Art, New York City, Annual Exhibition

1952 Mostra Triennale, Naples, Italy

Saidenberg Gallery, New York City

Whitney Museum of American Art, New York City, Annual Exhibition

1953 Carnegie Museum, Pittsburgh, Carnegie International

Whitney Museum of American Art, New York City, Annual Exhibition

1954 Alan Gallery, New York City

Hunter College, New York City

The Solomon R. Guggenheim Museum, New York City, "Younger American Painters"

1955 Corcoran Gallery of Art, Washington, D. C. Twenty-fourth Biennial Exhibition

University of Illinois, Urbana, "Contemporary American Painting"

Whitney Museum of American Art, New York City, "The New Decade: Thirty-five Painters and Sculptors"

REFERENCES

The entries are arranged in chronological order in each section.

EXHIBITION CATALOGUES

Catalogue of an exhibition at the 67 Gallery, New York City, 1945.

Attilio Salemme. Catalogue of an exhibition at the Julius Carlebach Gallery, New York City, 1947.

Hale, Robert Beverly, ed. *American Painting Today.* Catalogue of an exhibition at The Metropolitan Museum of Art, New York City, 1950.

Attilio Salemme. Catalogue of an exhibition at the Saidenberg Gallery, New York City, 1952.

Attilio Salemme. Catalogue of an exhibition at the Grace Borgenicht Gallery, New York City, 1953.

Sweeney, James Johnson. *Younger American Painters.* Catalogue of an exhibition at The Solomon R. Guggenheim Museum, New York City, 1954.

Attilio Salemme, 1911-1955. Catalogue of an exhibition at the Duveen-Graham Gallery, New York City, 1955.

Contemporary American Painting and Sculpture. Catalogue of an exhibition at the University of Illinois, Urbana, 1955.

Baur, John I. H., ed. *The New Decade: 35 American Painters and Sculptors.* Catalogue of an exhibition at the Whitney Museum of American Art, New York City, 1955.

Messer, Thomas M., and John I. H. Baur. *Attilio Salemme.* Catalogue of an exhibition at the Institute of Contemporary Art, Boston, 1959.

Attilio Salemme: Selected Paintings 1944-1955. Catalogue of an exhibition at the Staempfli Gallery, New York City, 1962.

Attilio Salemme: Paintings and Works on Paper 1942-1955. Catalogue of an exhibition at the André Emmerich Gallery, New York City, 1974.

NEWSPAPERS AND PERIODICALS

Riley, Maude. "Salemme Debut." *Art Digest* 19 (January 1, 1945): 9.

"Attilio Salemme." *Art News* 43 (January 15, 1945): 28.

"Attilio Salemme." *Art News* 45 (July 1946): 47.

"Salemme in the Village." *Art Digest* 20 (July 1, 1946): 20.

"Attilio Salemme." *Art News* 46 (September 1947): 38.

Reed, Judith Kaye. "Attilio Salemme Abstracts His Own World." *Art Digest* 21 (September 15, 1947): 11.

Boswell, Peyton, Jr. "Chicago Surveys the Abstract and Surrealist Art of America." *Art Digest* 22 (November 15, 1947): 9-10.

"U. S. Moderns Afloat." *Art News* 46 (January 1948): 35.

"Attilio Salemme." *Magazine of Art* 41 (March 1948): 97.

E. B. "Art on the High Seas." *Architectural Forum* 88 (April 1948): 152.

"Attilio Salemme." *Art News* 47 (April 1948): 59.

Gibbs, Josephine. "Clean-Cut Salemme." *Art Digest* 22 (April 15, 1948): 19.

"Modern Artes to Sea." *Fortune* 39 (June 1949): 95.

Reed, Judith Kaye. "Post-Mondrian Painters in Thoughtful Show." *Art Digest* 23 (June 1, 1949): 14.

Krasne, Belle. "New Gallery's Curtain Raiser." *Art Digest* 24 (March 15, 1950): 19.

Hale, Robert Beverly. "A Report on American Painting Today, 1950." *Metropolitan Museum of Art Bulletin* 9 (February 1951): 172.

"Met Buys Seven Oils from its Show." *Art Digest* 25 (February 15, 1951): 7.

Genauer, Emily. "Is There an American Style in Art?" *House Beautiful* 93 (June 1951): 93.

Louchheim, Aline B. "Art in New York Apartment." *New York Times,* July 29, 1951, p. 5.

Campbell, Larry. "Attilio Salemme." *Art News* 50 (January 1952): 42.

Fitz-simmons, James. "Attilio Salemme." *Art Digest* 26 (February 1, 1952): 18.

Kramer, Hilton. "Attilio Salemme." *Art Digest* 28 (October 15, 1953): 20.

Goodnough, Robert. "Attilio Salemme." *Art News* 52 (November 1953): 57.

Crehan, Hubert. "A Collection That's a Relief." *Art Digest* 28 (April 15, 1954): 6.

Crehan, Hubert. "Too Many Cooks." *Art Digest* 28 (May 1, 1954): 20.

Gordon, John. "Tomorrow." *The Brooklyn Museum Bulletin* 17 (1955): 26.

"Attilio Salemme." *Art News* 54 (March 1955): 7.

Tyler, Parker. "Attilio Salemme." *Art News* 54 (May 1955): 47.

Kreider, Stanton. "57th Street's Lonely Man." *Pictures on Exhibit* 18 (May 1955): 8-9.

Rosenblum, Robert. "Attilio Salemme." *Art Digest* 29 (May 1, 1955): 22.

Johnson, Una E. "Contemporary American Painters: Attilio Salemme, Painter and Draftsman." *Perspectives U.S.A.* 13 (Autumn 1955): 96.

Burrows, Carlyle. "Art Institute Gives Salemme Memorial." *New York Herald Tribune,* September 7, 1958.

Campbell, Lawrence. "Salemme: Figures From a Private World." *Art News* 58 (April 1959): 32-33, 51.

"The Sad Doorman." *Time,* April 6, 1959, p. 76.

Coates, Robert M. "The Salemme Memorial." *New Yorker,* April 25, 1959, pp. 103-4.

Schiff, Bennett. "In the Art Galleries..." *New York Post,* May 3, 1959.

Getlein, Frank. "Inside and Outside: Miró and Salemme." *The New Republic,* May 25, 1959, p. 22.

Breuning, Margaret. "The Salemme Retrospective." *Arts Magazine 33 (June 1959): 52.*

Schwartz, M. D. *"Attilio Salemme at the Whitney Museum." Apollo* 70 (July 1959): 6.

Burckhardt, Edith. "Attilio Salemme." *Art News* 59 (May 1960): 13.

Tillim, Sidney. "Attilio Salemme." *Arts Magazine* 34 (June 1960): 53.

Collins, H. F. "Attilio Salemme, Socialist Surrealist." *Scholastic Arts* 60 (January 1961): 38-39.

Campbell, Lawrence. "Attilio Salemme." *Art News* 61 (December 1962): 54.

Judd, Donald. "Attilio Salemme." *Arts Magazine* 37 (January 1963): 55.

Hooton, Bruce, D. "Attilio Salemme." *Art News* 66 (February 1968): 16.

"Salemme at Terry Dintenfass." *Arts Magazine* 42 (February 1968): 23.

Pincus-Witten, Robert. "Attilio Salemme." *Artforum* 8 (February 1970): 73.

Kline, Katherine. "Attilio Salemme." *Art News* 68 (February 1970): 62.

Frackman, Noel. "Attilio Salemme." *Arts Magazine* 49 (September 1974): 55.

LENDERS TO THE EXHIBITION

The Brooklyn Museum, New York, New York
Mrs. James E. Cross, Chicago, Illinois
Dr. and Mrs. Graham G. Hawks, New York, New York
Mr. and Mrs. Joseph Kaufman, New York, New York
The Metropolitan Museum of Art, New York, New York
Mr. Ben Mildwoff, New York, New York
The Museum of Modern Art, New York, New York
Philadelphia Museum of Art, Pennsylvania
Mrs. Attilio Salemme, New York, New York, and her sons, Vincent and Lawrence Salemme
The Solomon R. Guggenheim Museum, New York, New York
Whitney Museum of American Art, New York, New York

CATALOGUE OF THE EXHIBITION

Unless otherwise indicated, the paintings listed below were lent by the artist's widow, Mrs. Attilio Salemme, and her sons, Vincent and Lawrence Salemme.

All works are oil on canvas.

Dimensions are in inches, followed in parentheses by centimeters. Height precedes width.

1. **SELF-PORTRAIT** 1940   25 x 20 (63.5 x 50.8)

2. **LEAF ABSTRACTION** 1942   25 x 15 (63.5 x 38.1)

3. **STILL-LIFE WITH RED WALL** 1942 25 x 30 (63.5 x 76.2)

4. **THE CALM ENCOUNTER OF PUGNACIOUS CHARACTERS** 1943
   20 x 43 (50.8 x 109.2)

5. **IN THE WORLD OF STILL-LIFE** 1944
   30 x 36 (76.2 x 91.4)

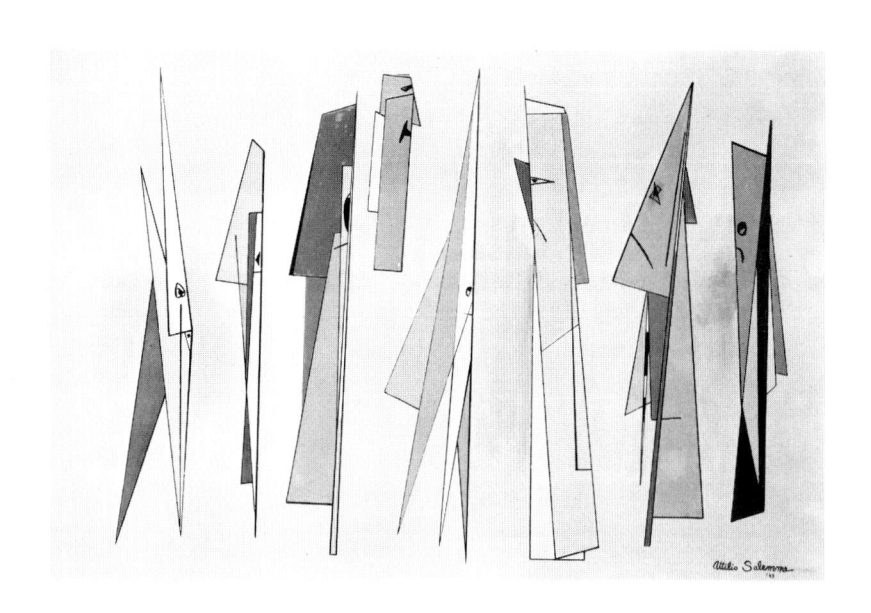

6. **LABYRINTHIAN CITY** 1944   33 x 43 (83.8 x 109.2)

7. **THE WOMB OF TIME** 1944 32 x 50 (81.3 x 126.9)

Lent by Dr. and Mrs. Graham G. Hawks, New York, New York

8. **NOSTALGIA OF PURITY** 1944   33 x 43 (83.8 x 109.2)

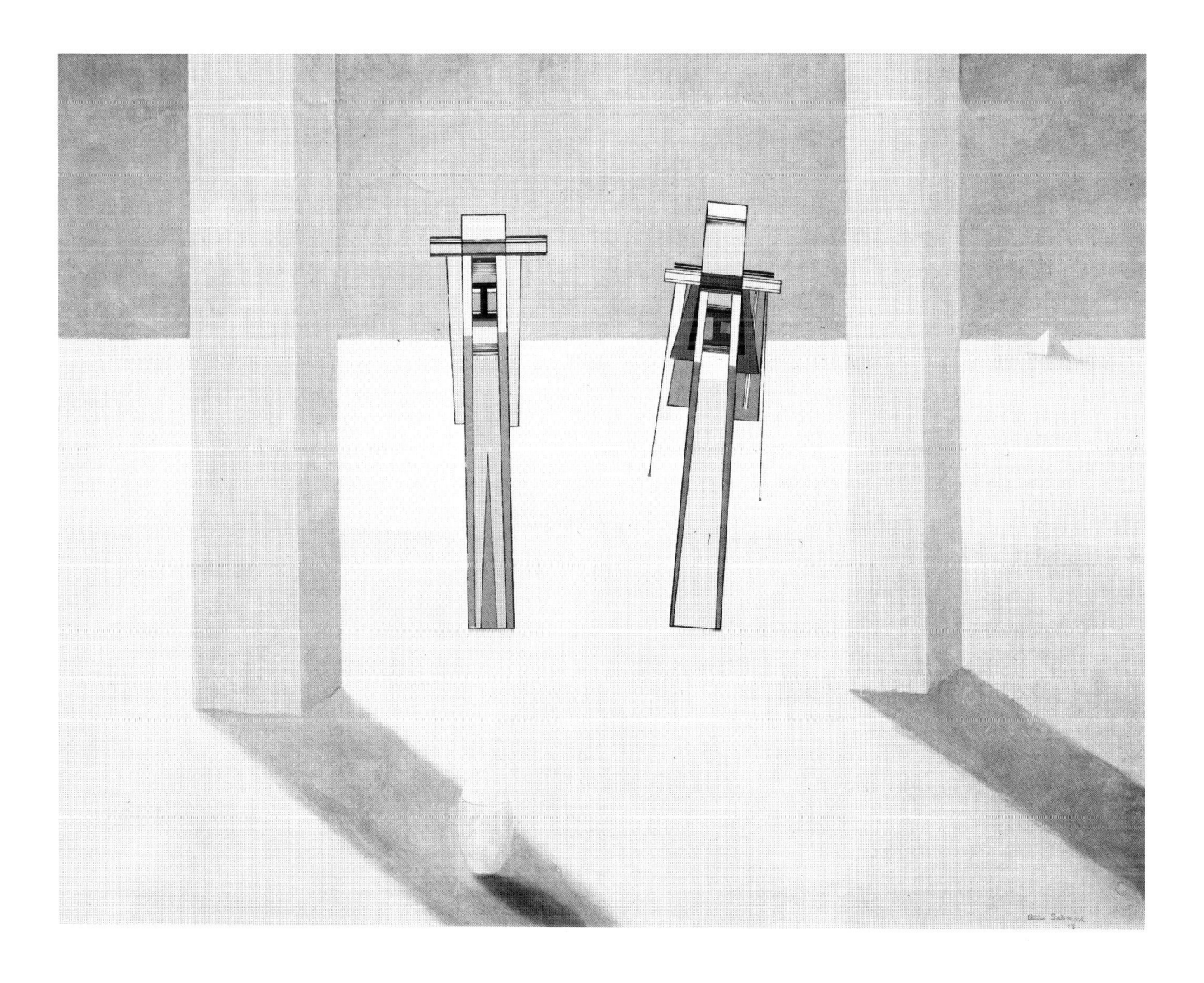

9. **ATAVISTIC PREMONITION** 1944   16 x 20 (40.6 x 50.8)   10. **THE INESCAPABLE CONSCIOUSNESS** 1944   20 x 30 (50.8 x 76.2)

Anonymous lender

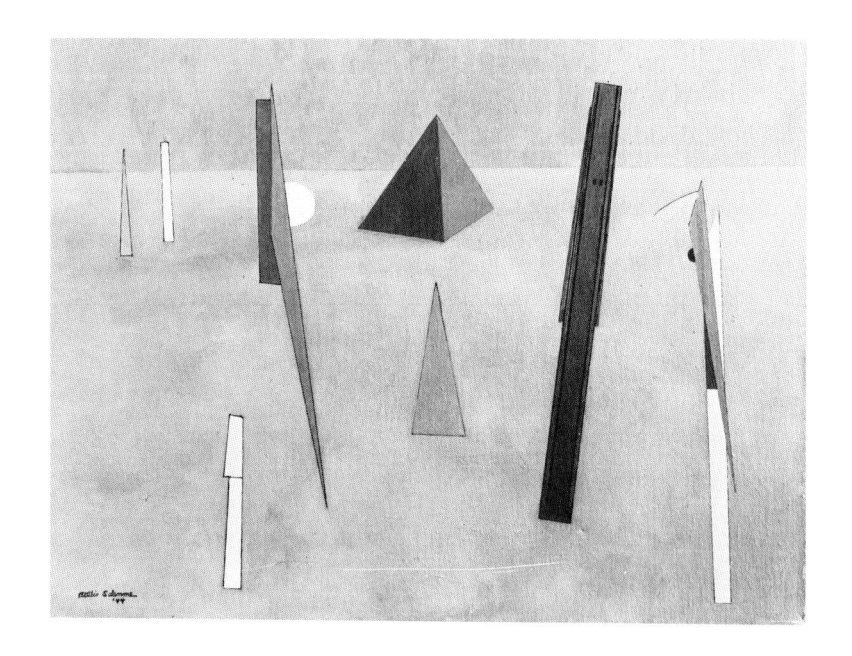

30

11. **ASTRONOMICAL EXPERIMENT** 1945   30 x 40 (76.2 x 101.6)

*Lent by The Museum of Modern Art, New York, New York; Gift of
Mrs. John D. Rockefeller 3rd*

12. **ECHO OF A DREAM** 1945   22 x 40 (55.8 x 101.6) 13. **LONELY INHABITANT OF A DREAM** 1945   21 x 45 (53.3 x 114.3)

Lent by Mrs. James E. Cross, Chicago, Illinois

14. **THE FINAL VICTORY** 1945   25 x 15 (63.5 x 38.1)

15. **THROUGH THE STUDIO** 1946 ` 28 x 43 (71.1 x 109.2)

16. **JOYS OF THE ARCHITECT** 1946 14 x 30 (35.5 x 76.2)

Lent by Whitney Museum of American Art, New York, New York; Gift of Mr. and Mrs. Jules Reiner

17. **ENIGMA OF JOY** 1947 (Frontispiece) 52 x 80 (132 x 203.2)

National Collection of Fine Arts; Gift of the National Maritime Association

18. **TOMORROW** 1947 19 x 36 (45.7 x 91.4)

Lent by The Brooklyn Museum, New York; Dick S. Ramsey Fund

19. **ASYMPTOTE OF MAGIC** 1947   42 x 63 (106.7 x 160)

*Lent by The Solomon R. Guggenheim Museum, New York,
New York; Gift of Lucia Autorino*

20. **AFTERNOON IN INFINITY** 1947   29 x 36 (73.7 x 91.4)

Lent by Mr. and Mrs. Joseph Kaufman, New York, New York

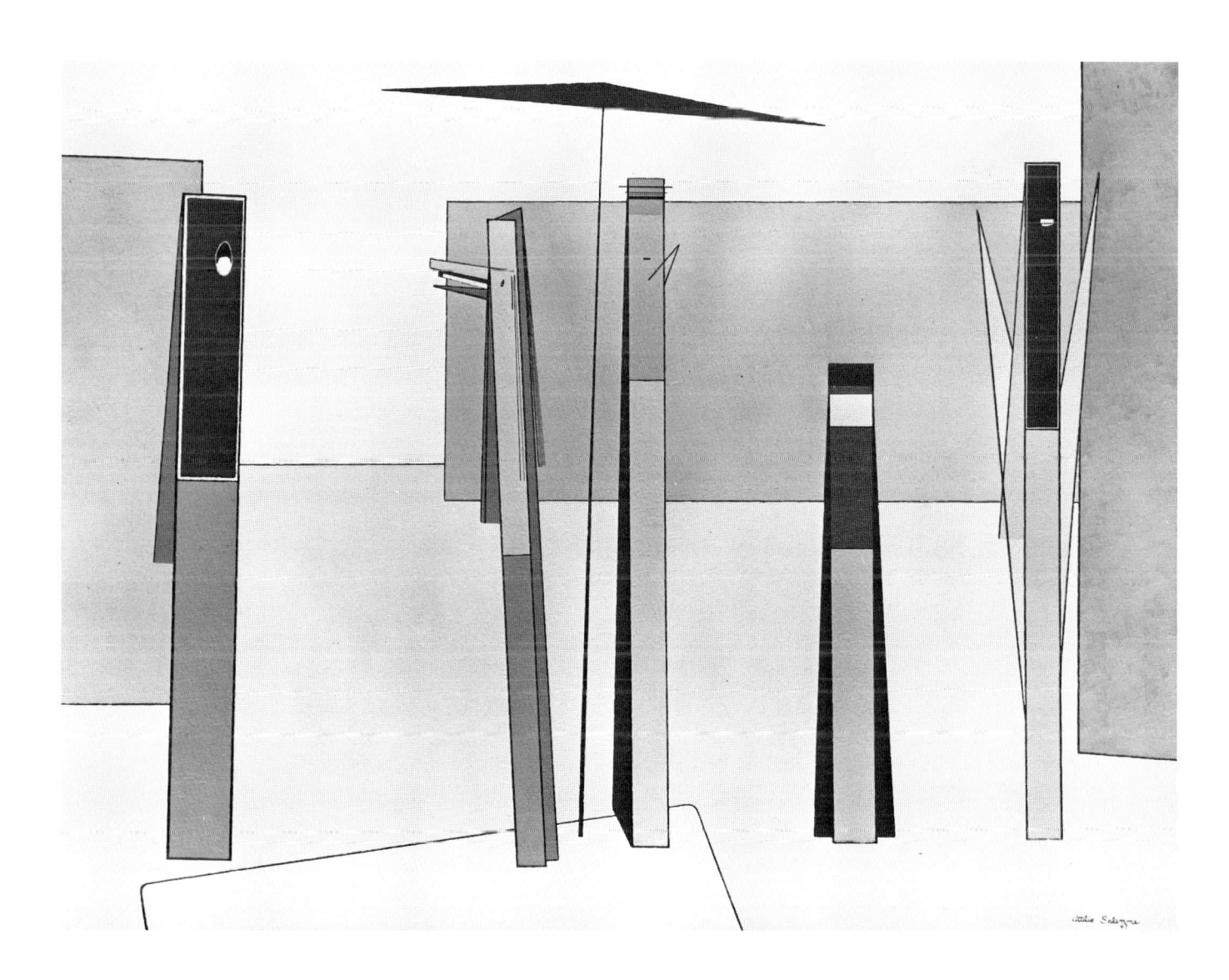

21. **NIGHT OF THE RITUAL** 1947   40 x 60 (101.6 x 152.3)

22. **TRAGEDY** 1947   30 x 43 (76.2 x 109.2)

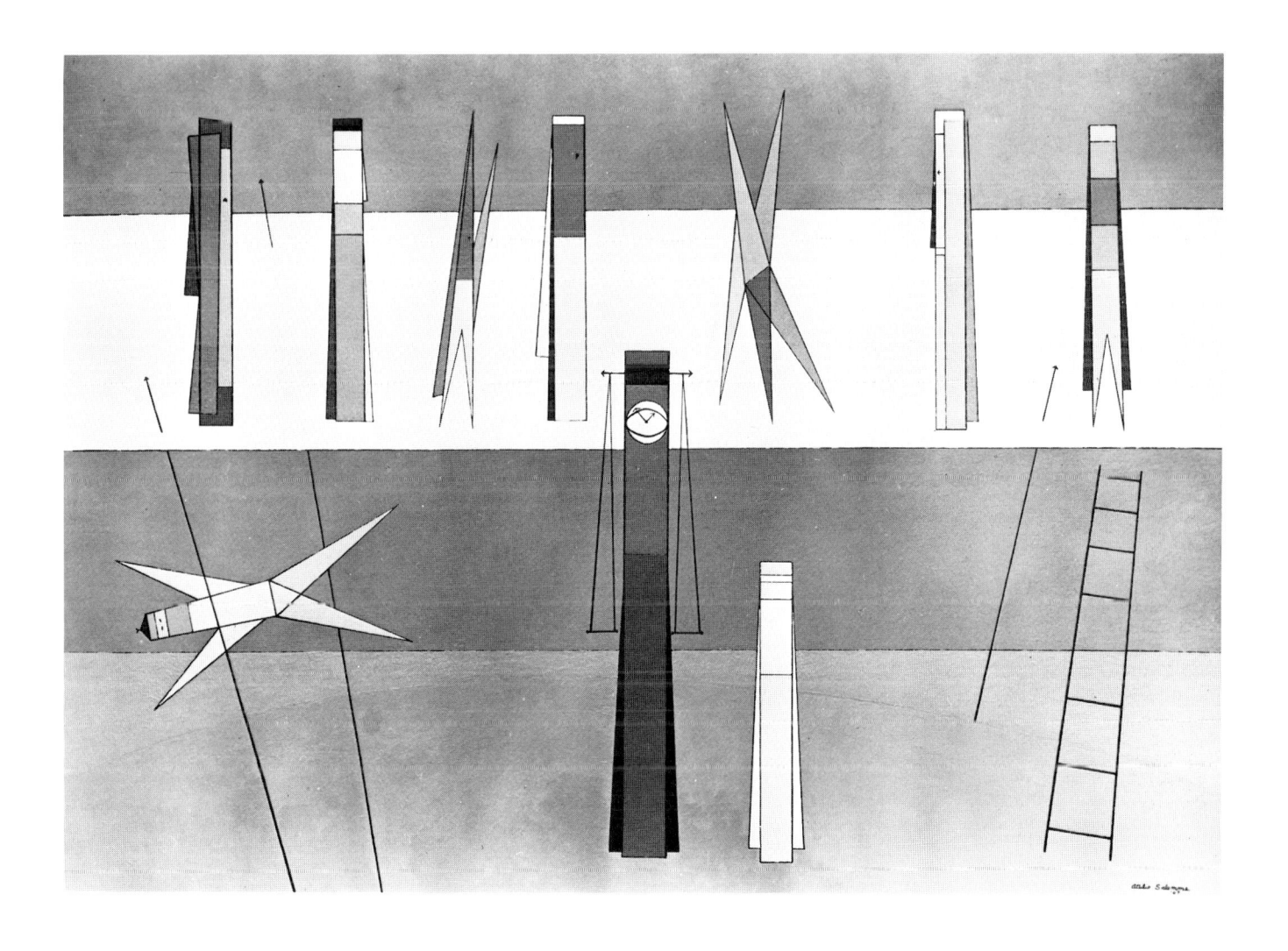

23. **FROM NADIR TO ZENITH** 1948   42 x 66 (106.6 x 167.5)

24. **SCHOOL FOR DIPLOMATS** 1948   34 x 44 (86.4 x 111.7)

25. RETURN OF THE ANGEL 1948   14 x 23 (35.5 x 58.4)

*Lent by Whitney Museum of American Art, New York, New York;
Gift of Mr. and Mrs. Daniel Saidenberg*

26. **REVELATION** 1948   30 x 41 (76.2 x 104.1)

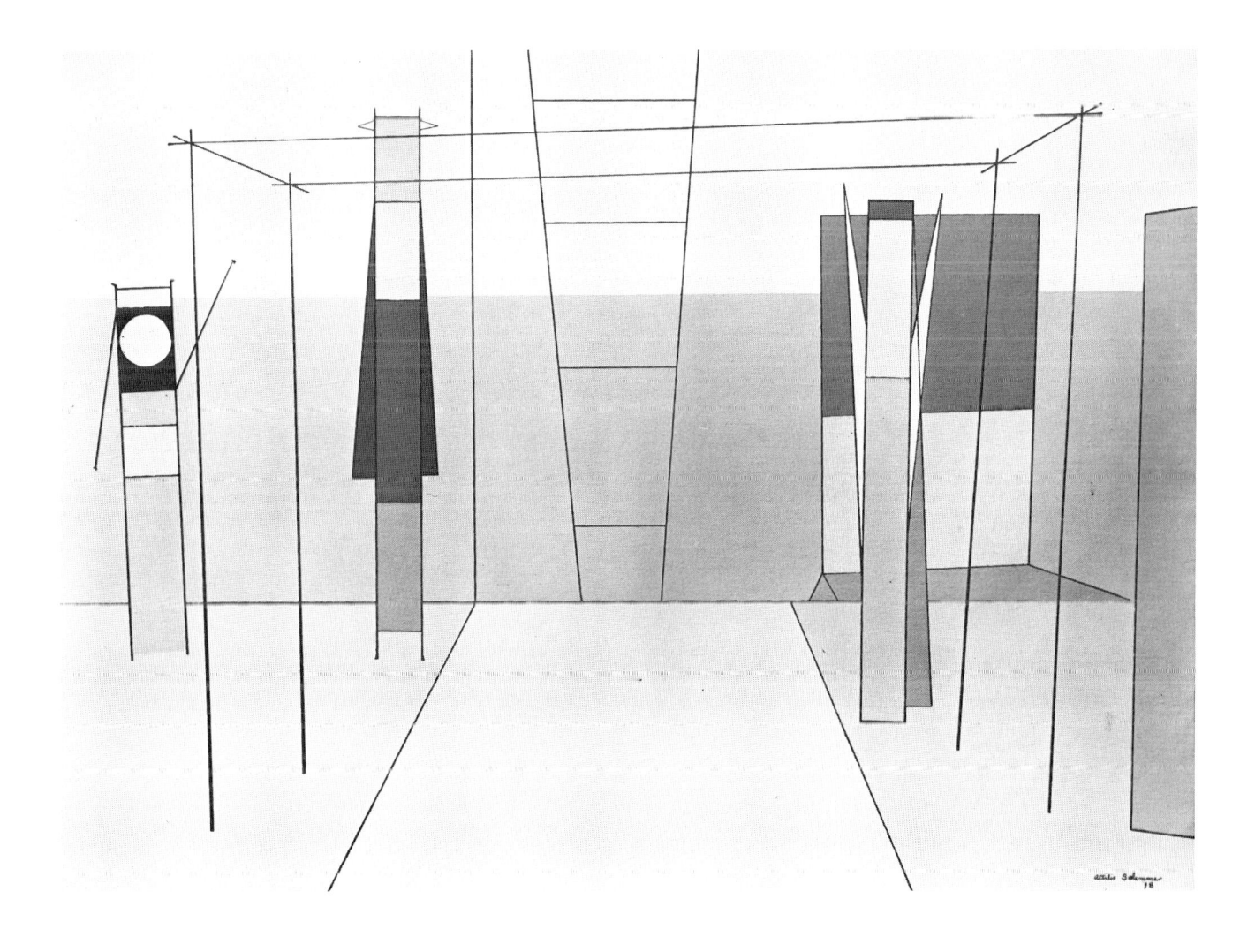

27. **VINTAGE OF UNCERTAINTIES** 1949   16 x 42 (40.6 x 106.6)

Lent by Mr. Ben Mildwoff, New York, New York

28. **INTO THE NIGHT** 1949 (Cover)   21 x 14 (53.3 x 35.5)

29. **STUDY FOR MURAL, FRA ANGELICO** 1949-50   13 x 42 (33 x 106.6)

30. **STUDY FOR MURAL, IN THE MIRROR OF THE SEA** 1949   13 x 43 (33 x 109.2)

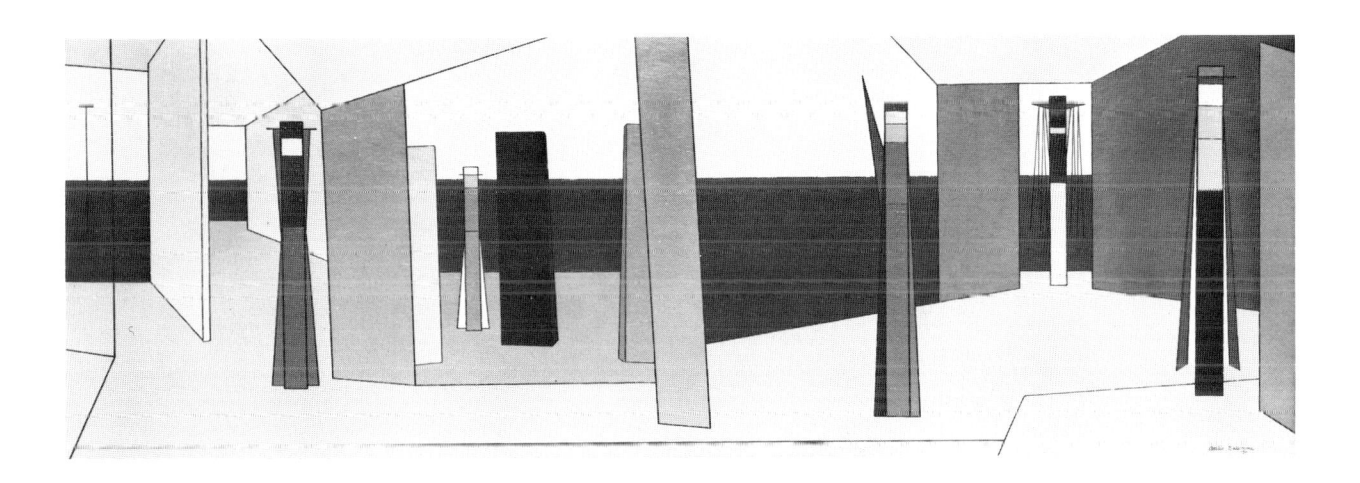

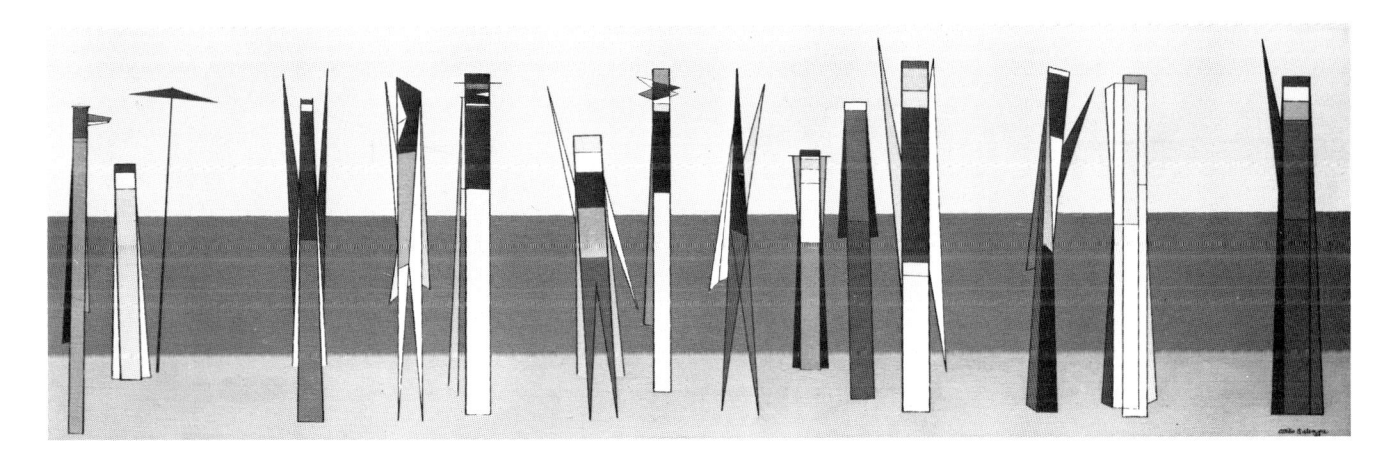

31. **THE ORACLE** 1950 48 x 72 (121.8 x 182.8)

Lent by Philadelphia Museum of Art; Gift of Mrs. H. Gates Lloyd

32. **THE SACRIFICE** 1950 60 x 80 (152.3 x 203.2)

33. **GREEK ELEGY** 1951   42 x 34 (106.6 x 86.4)

34. **DAWN BALLET** 1951   28 x 50 (71.1 x 126.9)

Lent by The Solomon R. Guggenheim Museum, New York, New York; Gift of Willard Svanoe

35. **THE BATTLE** 1951   28 x 40 (71.1 x 101.6)

36. **THE FAMILY** 1952   38 x 28 (96.5 x 71.1)

37. **FRIENDLY RELATIVES** 1952 38 x 28 (96.5 x 71.1)

38. **GRAND INTERIOR AND SEPARATION** 1952 52 x 80 (132 x 203.2)

39. **THE INQUISITION** 1952   40 x 63 (101.6 x 160)

*Lent by Whitney Museum of American Art, New York, New York;
Gift of Mr. and Mrs. Jules Reiner*

40. **BEAUTIES OF THE SQUARE** 1952   32 x 43 (81.3 x 109.2)

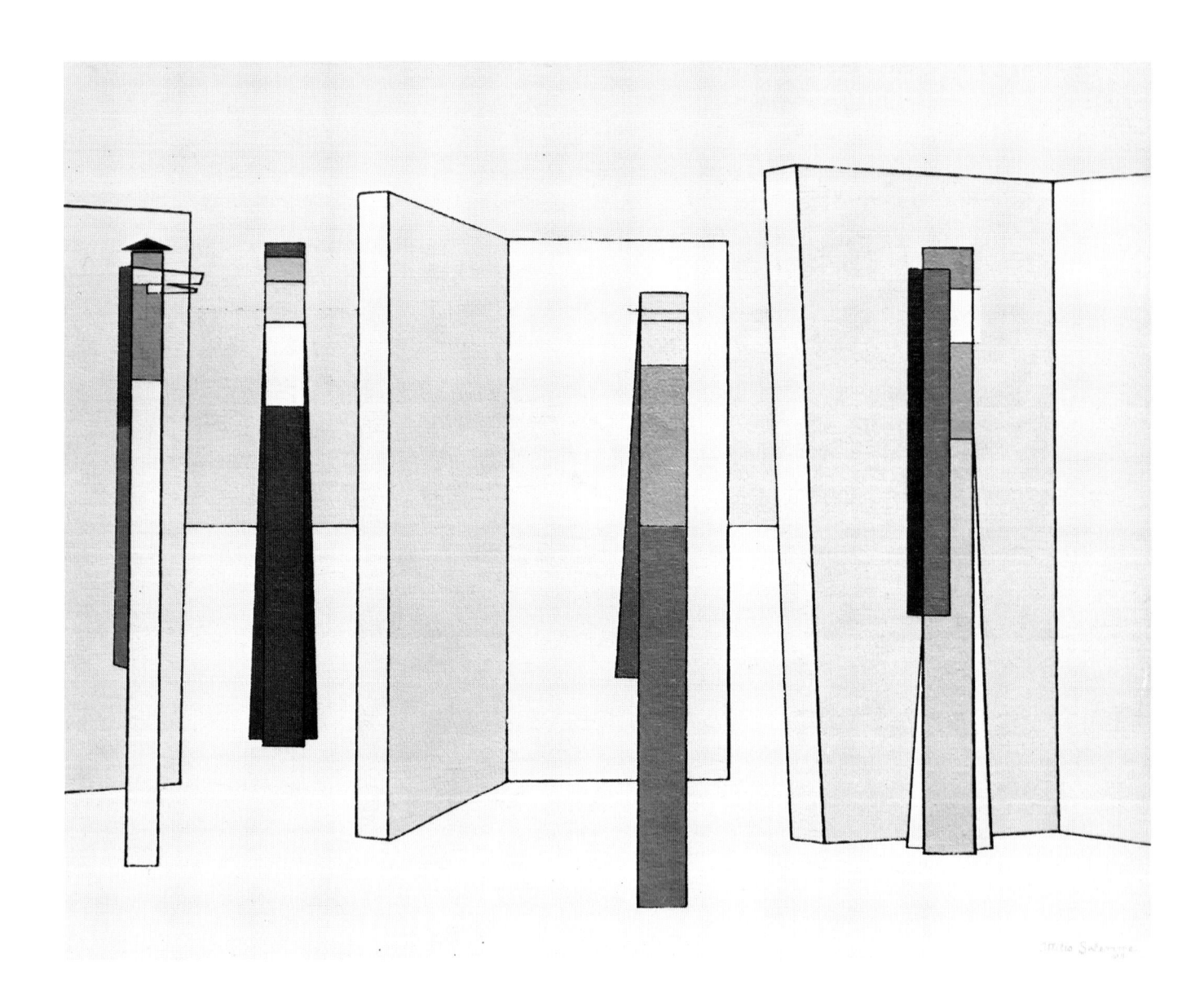

41. **DOUBTS OF THE AFTERNOON** 1952   64 x 80 (162.5 x 203.2)

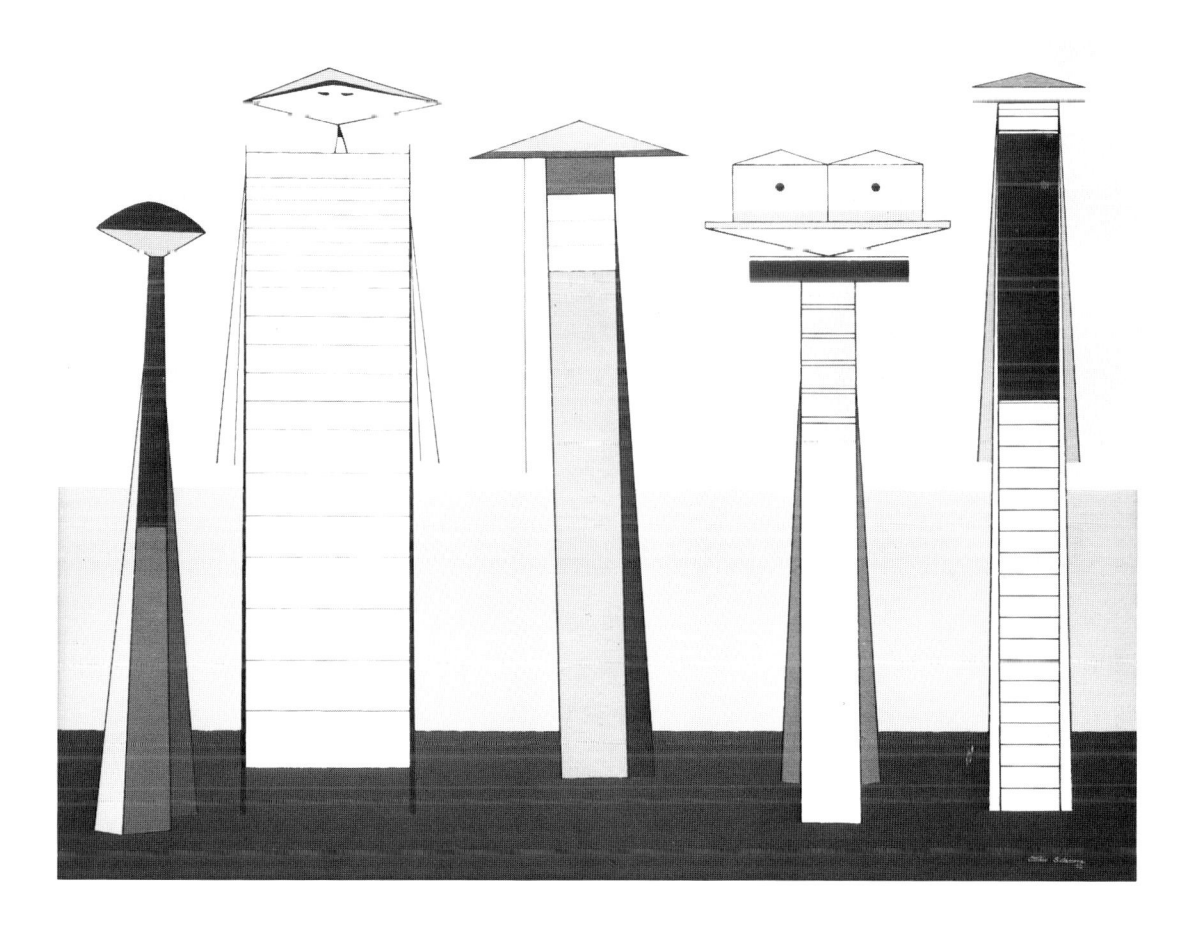

42. **MAHATMAS OF THE LUNAR SHORE** 1953   52 x 80 (132 x 203.2)

43. **CAUGHT IN THE EQUINOX** 1953   52 x 80 (132 x 203.2)

*Lent by The Metropolitan Museum of Art, New York, New York;
Arthur H. Hearn Fund, 1953*

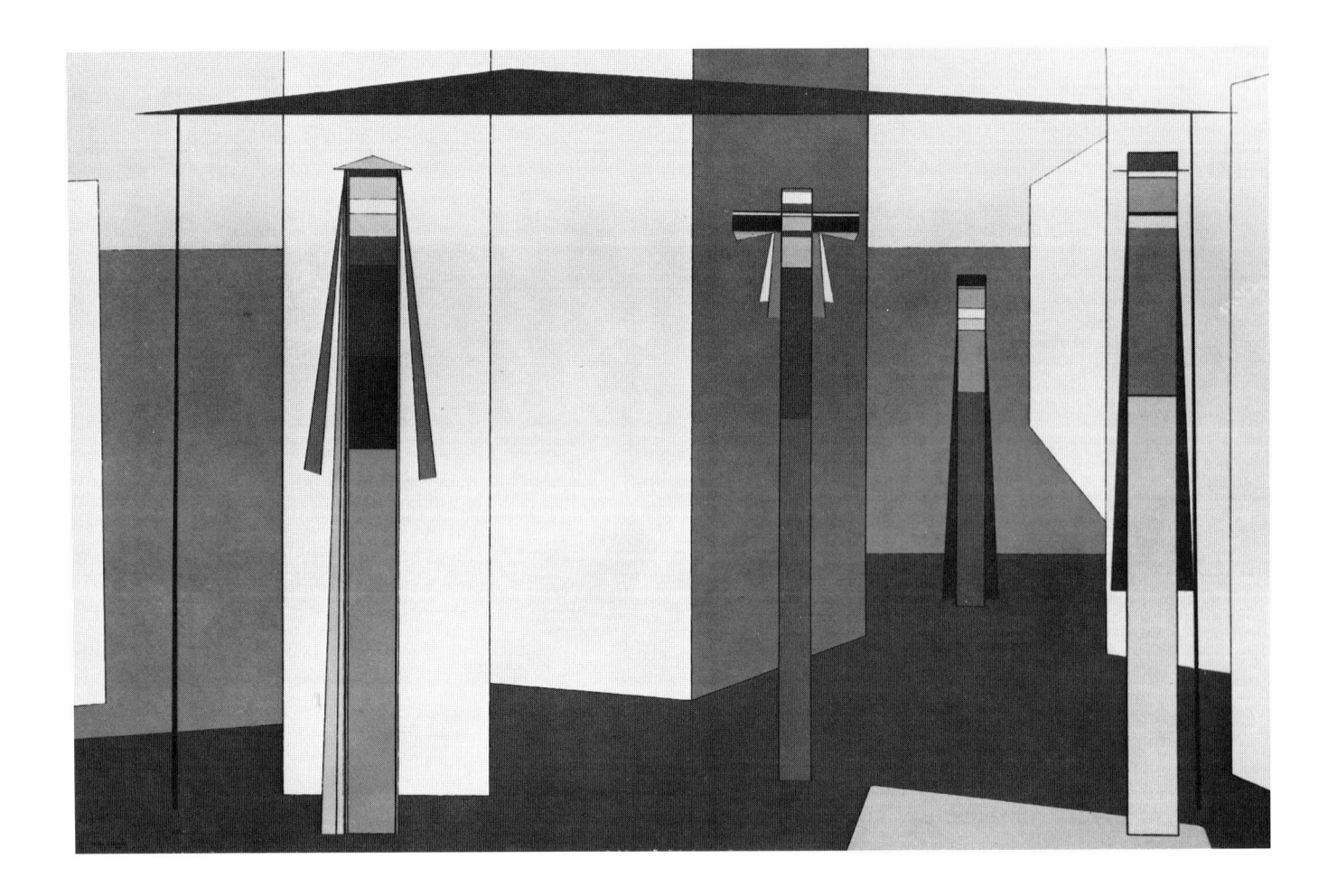

44. LUNAR VOYAGE 1954   24 x 36 (60.9 x 91.4)

*Lent by The Solomon R. Guggenheim Museum of Art, New York,
New York; Gift of Dennis Paddock.*

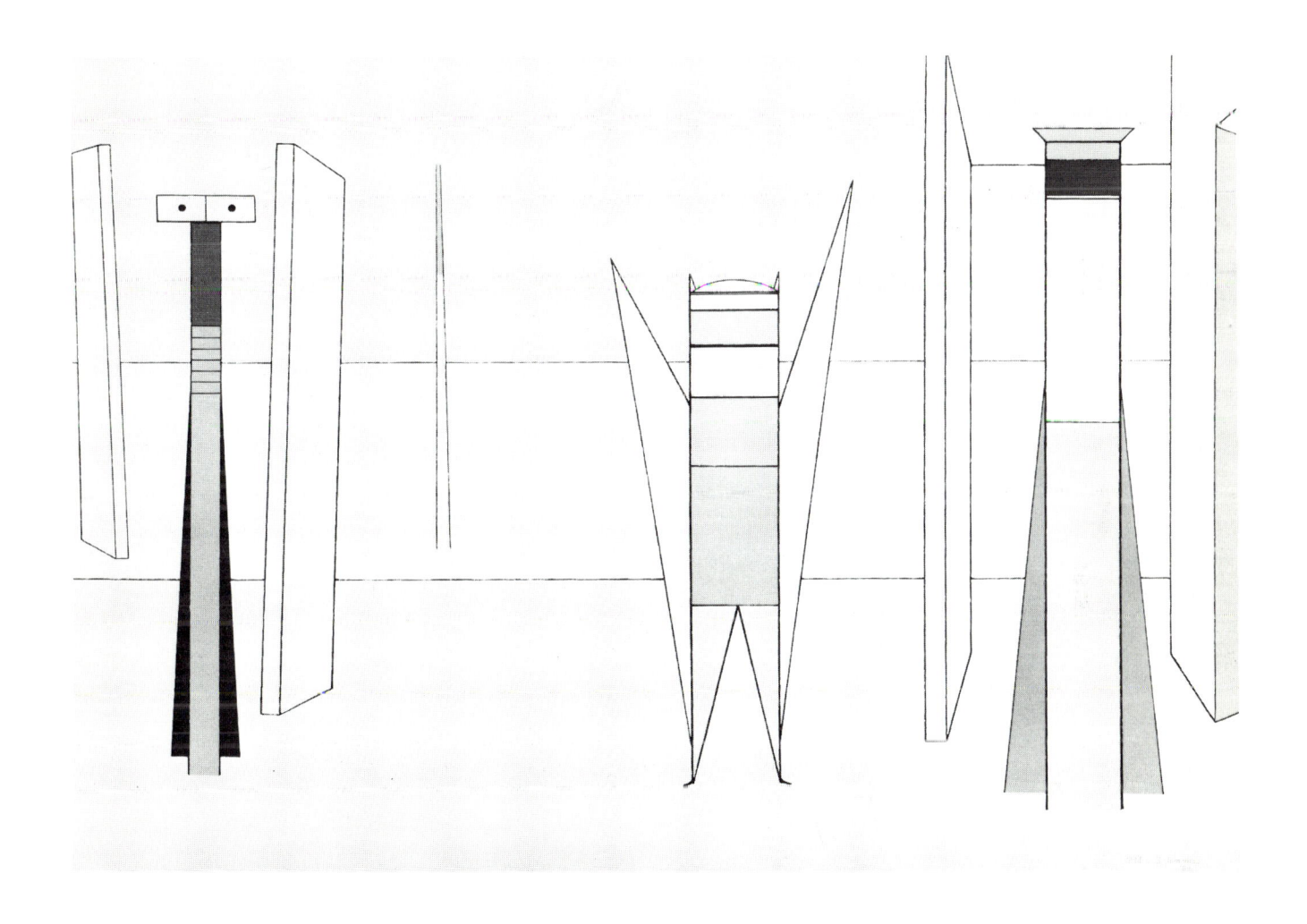

45. **SORORITY OF LIBIDINOUS LIBRAS** 1954   40 x 60 (101.6 x 152.3)

46. **ADAM AND EVE** 1954   30 x 20 (76.2 x 50.8)

47. **ASTRO-PHYSICS EXPERIMENT** 1954   24 x 36 (60.9 x 91.4)

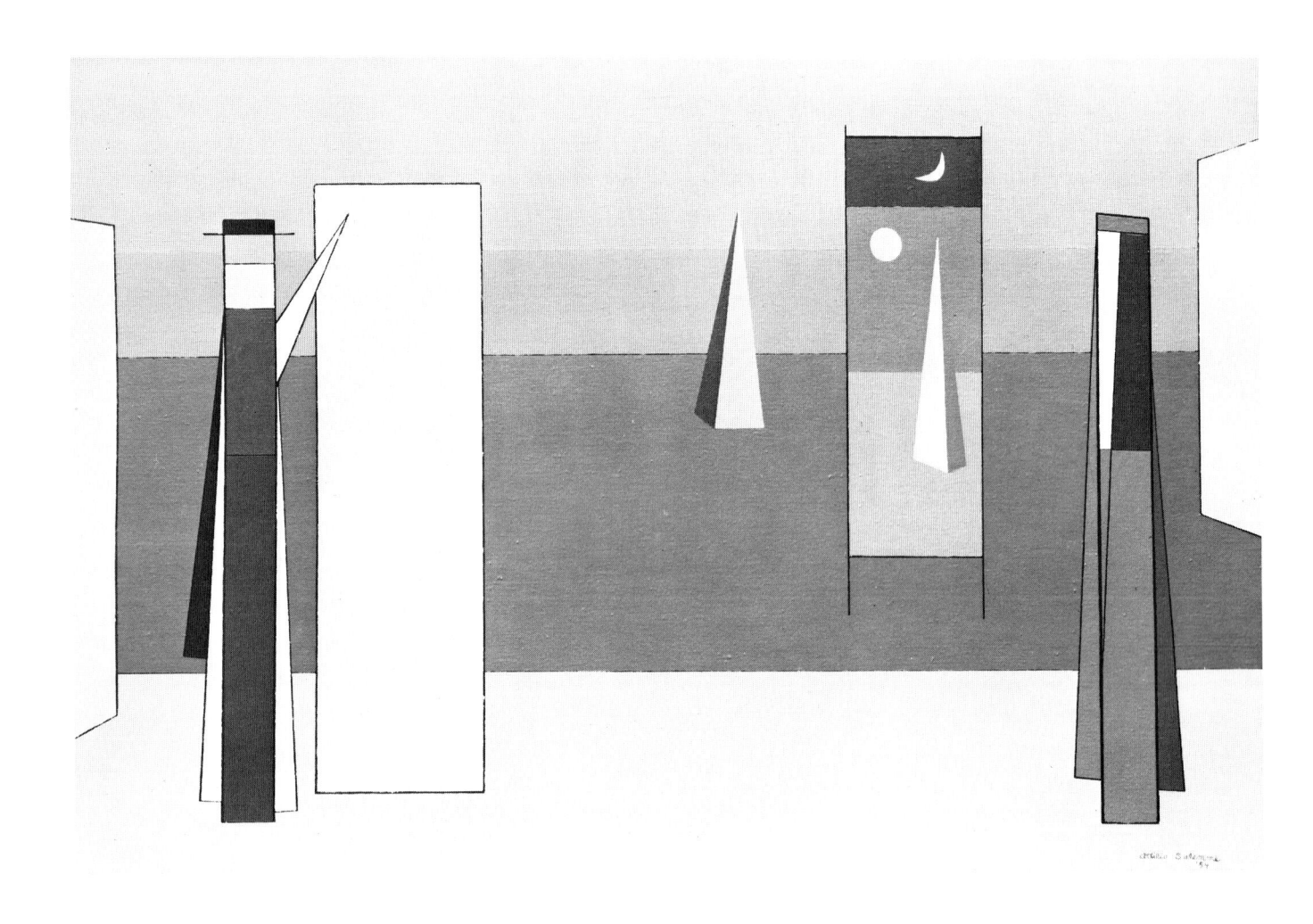

48. **ENGINEER IN THE KINDERGARTEN** 1954   17 x 43 (43.2 x 109.2)

49. **THE HOLIDAY** 1954   15 x 21 (38.1 x 53.3)

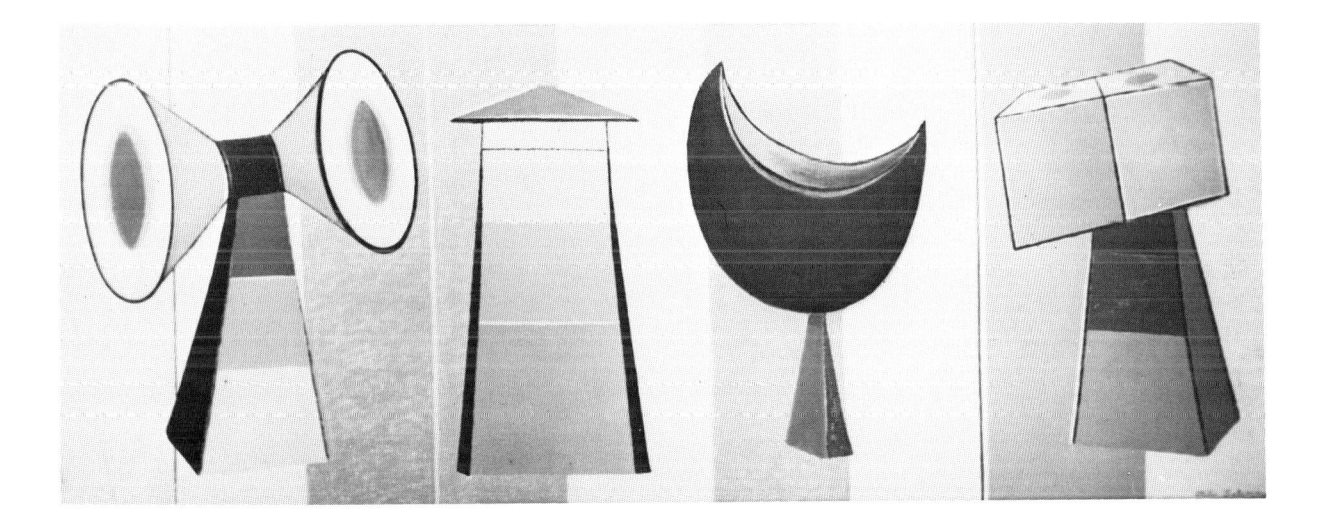

50. **MME. X** 1955 40 x 60 (101.6 x 152.3)

DATE LOANED